GIRL, YOU'RE NOT CRAZY. YOU'RE DEALING WITH A NARCISSIST

GIRL, YOU'RE NOT CRAZY. YOU'RE DEALING WITH A NARCISSIST

CAROLYN BOOKER-PIERCE

J. Merrill
PUBLISHING

ISBN: 978-1-950719-40-2 (Paperback)

ISBN: 978-1-950719-41-9 (eBook)

J Merrill Publishing, Inc.
434 Hillpine Drive
Columbus, OH 43207

www.JMerrillPublishingInc.com

CONTENTS

INTRODUCTION

If you have ever found yourself in a relationship with a self-absorbed, self-centered, and a person who lacks empathy and emotion, you are not alone. Many people have found themselves dealing with that type of person too. That person is a narcissist. I don't know if you were like me, a person who dreamed of marrying Mr. Right or for the man who may be reading the book, Mrs. Right. I started by dating the guys from my fairytale list. You know, from the tall, dark, and handsome to the rich, loaded man, I thought I would be proud to call my true love.

That list had the guy who drove the fancy car and likes to wine and dine. That guy would make me smile by telling me everything I wanted to hear like he loved me and would take good care of me. That is the guy most women would love, including me, because everyone thought that would be a great guy. However, many times that guy I thought was great would end up making me cry. That guy would make promises that I would get excited about, but he would not keep. Just when I thought I was in a good relationship, he would disappear or move on without giving me proper notice. Even if he did not move on physically, he would move on emotionally or never fully committed in the first place. It wasn't long into my adulthood that I realized most of my dreams would turn into nightmares. It seemed like I was always picking the wrong guys, but in reality, I tend to always fall for the narcissist.

Who wouldn't? Narcissists tend to be charming promising to make all of your dreams come true. Narcissists initially are loved by all of your family and friends. Most narcissists on the surface have great personalities. Narcissists are easy to fall in love with. Not so easy to stay in love with. Narcissists will tell you a lie and try to convince you the sky is red when it is blue. They will tell you something one day and swear they didn't say it the next day. A narcissist will tell you, girl, you are crazy when, in fact, what you heard them say or saw them do is really true.

I am not blaming all men or narcissists for my failed relationships. I have learned to take responsibility for the choices I make. I have learned that I can't ignore the red flags. That includes knowing when a man has had several failed relationships in the past that I should not have assumed it would be different with me. Common sense should tell me if a man was unfaithful more than once. However, I was not being responsible by staying in an unhealthy relationship once I knew the truth. When the narcissist showed me who he was, I should have believed him. If a man did not pay his own bills, I know this doesn't make any sense in hindsight that I thought he would pay his bills with me.

When a man apologized for a promise broken, I would thank God this is not going to happen again, but with the narcissist, it did. When I thought I would be first or even considered first in a "committed" relationship, it would not be long before finding out the man was selfish and only thought of himself. Considering my feelings while in a relationship with a narcissist was not on the narcissist's radar. I thought surely the man of my dreams would change and consider my needs if I just loved and supported him more. Wrong. This is especially not true when dealing with a narcissist.

Does any of this sound familiar? Men are not the only ones who exhibit this type of personality disorder. Let's be clear there are many female narcissists in the world. However, studies have shown around 80% of narcissists tend to be men. Most of my narcissistic encounters have been with males, with only a few females that showed narcissistic behaviors. That is why I will be talking more from a female perspective with narcissistic males. However, you can use the same information to spot a female narcissist. I have had more experience with male narcissists and have done more study on the male narcissist. Just keep in mind, regardless of being male or female, the main characteristics of a narcissist are self-absorbed, cannot empathize with others, and will try to make you think you are crazy.

WHAT IS A NARCISSIST?

To understand what you are dealing with, you must first know that some people with a trait known as a personality disorder. Wikipedia describes the narcissistic personality disorder[1] as this,

66 Narcissistic personality disorder is a personality disorder with a long-term pattern of abnormal behavior characterized by exaggerated feelings of self-importance, excessive need for admiration, and a lack of empathy. Those affected often spend much

time thinking about achieving power or success, or on their appearance. They often take advantage of the people around them. The behavior typically begins by early adulthood, and occurs across a variety of social situations. The cause of narcissistic personality disorder is unknown. It is a personality disorder classified within cluster B by the Diagnostic and Statistical Manual of Mental Disorders (DSM). Diagnosis is made by a healthcare professional interviewing the person in question. Then condition needs to be differentiated from mania and substances use disorder.

With all the above in mind one of things that stick out the most in reference to a narcissist would be the, *"long-term pattern of abnormal behavior characterized by exaggerated feelings of self-importance, excessive need for admiration, and a lack of empathy."* That sticks out to me because if you have ever been in a relationship with a narcissist like I have multiple times. You will learn it has always been about them; their need for attention and their lack of being able to care about others feelings. They are usually very self centered individuals who are determine to have life their way centered around what they want and need.

Bishop R.C. Blakes in his YouTube video "The Mind Games Narcissists Plays In Relationships[2]" I like the point he made in describing the behavior of the narcissist in relationships,

> Narcissists are the masters of confusion...you can pretty much determine that you are involved in a narcissistic connection be it romantic or friendly or whatever or familiar or family should I say. When you are dealing with a person on a simple subject that when they get through talking about it or interacting on it, you're confused.

He refers to the narcissist, as being like the

spirit of Lucifer in the garden when Satan confuses the women (Eve) and convinces her that God said she could eat from the forbidden tree. Then the woman confuses the man (Adam) in Genesis, the 3rd chapter. He says the whole thing falls apart. Listen to what Satan says in Genesis Chapter 3 verse 2-6,

> 2 *And the woman said unto the serpent, We may eat of the fruit of the trees of the garden:*
> 3 *But of the fruit of the tree which is in the midst of the garden, God hath said, Ye shall not eat of it, neither shall ye touch it, lest ye die.*
> 4 *And the serpent said unto the woman, Ye shall not surely die:*
> 5 *For God doth know that in the day ye eat thereof, then your eyes shall be opened, and ye shall be as gods, knowing good and evil.*

> *⁶ And when the woman saw that the tree was good for food, and that it was pleasant to the eyes, and a tree to be desired to make one wise, she took of the fruit thereof, and did eat, and gave also unto her husband with her; and he did eat.*

Satan charmed the woman with his lies, causing her to be confused about what God had said. Now he has not only caused her to separate from the one she loves, God. Satan's lies caused confusion with the women's husband, Adam. That is how narcissist manages to manipulate to get what they want. They will charm you by lying and making false promises; they do not intend to keep. Then they will leave you with consequences. Bishop went on to say this about the narcissist,

66 They can not see you as an individual

with feelings. They only view you as a means to an end.

Therefore try to remember when dealing with a narcissist, no matter how charming they may seem to be, their dominant characteristics are self-importance, self adsorbed, and they lack empathy.

2

PETER PAN, THE NARCISSIST

L et's look at the young man Peter Pan in the Peter Pan story that refuses to grow up as he relates to the narcissists. We can start by first seeing what Wikipedia says the about the Peter Pan syndrome[1],

> *Peter Pan syndrome is an inability to grow up or engage in behavior usually associated with adulthood. The term comes from the fictional children's character Peter Pan, who never ages. While transageism, or adults regarding themselves as juveniles or*

adolescents is not listed in the Diagnostic and Statistical Manual of Mental Disorders, and is not recognized by the American Psychiatric Association as a specific mental disorder, the concept is falsely modelled on transgenderism. This transageist concept has garnered a great deal of controversy. People who exhibit characteristics associated with the Peter Pan syndrome are sometimes referred to as Peter Panners.

Peter Pan, like the narcissist, looks to live life as an adventure. Instead of living a balanced, responsible life by working and making time to play. The mind of the narcissist and Peter Pan are irresponsible all play and no work, thus not capable of taking care of himself, let alone someone else. The bottom line is the narcissistic personality is an immature adult male who never grows up and is referred to as "Peter Pan." Peter Pans, like the narcissists, are emotionally immature and can't be forced to grow up. They can be very spontaneous, but they don't have a plan. They are big dreamers but somehow can't keep a real job. They are good at making promises, but they don't keep because when they made the promise, they never planned to ensure the promises made. Thus, when they are in an important intimate relationship, the female involved or vice versa are disappointed continuously, but the narcissist does not understand why. To the immature "Peter Pan narcissist," taking responsibility like keeping their word or not following through is not a big deal, at least not to them.

Women who are charmed by the Peter Pan or the narcissist are sucked in by their charm and elaborate stories they tell of how they are going to make all their dreams come true. Once the dream fails to manifest (which it will), the charming narcissist will move on with another bright idea that sounds just as charming as the first, all to blow it off as no big deal when he does not follow through. Yet, Peter Pan has left his true love feeling crazy for falling for it yet again.

(A side note to those who are asking why I have chosen to mainly use females as the victims of the narcissist in this writing, it is because studies have shown 75 to 80% of the narcissist are men).

Please don't misunderstand? I did not say 75 to 80% of men are narcissistic. I am saying out of the narcissistic personalities; the majority tend to be male. While fewer women have been identified as narcissistic personalities, know that some women do.

Usually, the narcissist's victim can't wrap her mind around why she is still being convinced there is hope for the immature narcissist to grow up. Why wouldn't he? She may say to herself. When, in fact, he only looks like a grown man. He is only a grown man in numbers. Maturity wise he is still a little boy still trying to play little boy games. Unfortunately, you may have become the game he is trying to play. Instead of holding "Peter Pan" accountable by not continuing to go along with his immature nonsense, women who I will refer to as Wendy Darling's, as depicted in the

Peter Pan story, enables Peter, the narcissist, by putting up with his immaturity.

Why do so many smart, educated, loving females fall for the Peter Pan or the narcissist? They fall for him because they love his charming ways. Like Wendy, who wants to take care of all the lost children while losing herself, so can we. I will talk more about Wendy in the next chapter and how she wants to believe Peter will change. But why would he change when he likes who he is? Peter Pan or narcissists are happy with his immature ways because, first of all, he doesn't understand he is immature. Peter Pan just wants to enjoy life and, most of the time, at others' expense. The narcissist most likely has never been held accountable by a parent, a spouse, and or his friends. Women who have chosen to stay with Peter Pan, the narcissist despite all the promises made and broken, the minimum wage jobs, and his desire to have fun in life and not plan for the future, have helped enable him most of the time. Therefore, to put all the blame on Peter Pan or the narcissist because you are not happy is not fair to Peter Pan or the narcissist. Women have chosen to stay with an immature narcissist like Peter Pan. I am not saying leave your narcissist, but don't expect him to grow up because you don't like his childish behavior. Remember, as Maya Angelo has said, "When someone shows you who they are, believe them."

3

ARE YOU A WENDY?

In the story of Peter Pan, Wendy is asked to take on the mother role for her brothers and Peter Pan. The phrase "Wendy syndrome[1]" is caring for others while failing to care for yourself. While it is essential to care for your partner, friends, and family, it is just as important to care for yourself. The unbalance comes when we put others' needs before our own. Those of us and I include myself because I am guilty of loving too much, and being like Wendy, I have like Wendy wanted to believe others will change if only we help them. I am very loyal to those I care about, and there are others like myself that have fallen into the "Wendy Syndrome" because of our loyalty to others. We find ourselves being mothers to grow men while not making sure our own needs are met. I am not saying don't be loyal, loving, and kind to your partner or your family and friends, you should. However, just don't forget to take care of yourself in the process.

When you are worried more about someone else's wellbeing while your own needs are not being met, it reminds me of something we all have heard when instructed by the stewardess if you've ever been on an airplane. They will tell you how to help yourself in the case of an emergency, "Put the mask on you first," which makes perfect sense. Why would you try to save someone else first and risk dying, when you can put the mask on you first, then try to help the person beside you so you both can live?

If this sounds like you, then you may suffer from the "Wendy Syndrome." You may struggle with the idea of not helping others first while despite putting yourself at risk. These people are innocent, caring people that just need to understand it is alright to take care of themselves first. I know that is hard to understand in a world that says your husband comes first, the children are first, and for those of the faith, the church comes first. However, how many women have you heard say I feel like I am losing it or I feel like I am going crazy? I know I have had the experience of both saying and feeling like I was going crazy. That then leaves the question, should we stop caring for our partners, children, family, and friends? Of course not! Like I said earlier, it is alright to care for others. Just make sure you take care of yourself first. If you don't, you may not be around to take care of Peter and all the other narcissists you love to take care of before yourself. If you suffer from codependency, you are more likely to fall into the "Wendy Syndrome." Codependents enable narcissists. *Elizabeth Cloud writes in chapter one of her book,* Codependency No More, *How to Cure Codependency, Start to Love Yourself and Fight for No More Codependent Relationship Ever,*

> *Every relationship has its ups and down. There are times when you will feel that you are so much in love, and there will also be times when that other person will disappoint you or hurt you. Just like the addictive behavior shown by addicts towards drugs, codependents have a similar kind of thing in relationships. The life of a codependent person is always around someone else, that is , the person or people they love. They do not know how to live for themselves, and their thoughts are always preoccupied with the people they love.*

These people are innocent, caring people that just need to understand it is alright to take care of themselves first. I know that is hard to understand in a world that says your husband comes first, the children are first, and for those of the faith, the church comes first. However, how many women have you heard say I feel like I am losing it or I feel like I am going crazy? I know I have had the experience of both saying and feeling like I was going crazy. That then leaves the question, should we stop caring for our partners, children, family, and friends? Of course not! Like I said earlier, it is alright to care for others. Just make sure you take care of yourself first. If you don't, you may not be around to take care of Peter and all the other narcissists you love to take care of before yourself. If you suffer from codependency, you are more likely to fall into the "Wendy Syndrome." Codependents enable narcissists. Wikipedia describes codependency[2] as a behavioral condition,

> Codependency is a behavioral condition in a relationship where one person enables another person's addiction, poor mental health, immaturity, irresponsibility, or under-achievement. Among the core characteristics of codependency is an excessive reliance on other people for approval and a sense of identity. Definitions of codependency vary, but it is generally defined as a

subclinical, situational, and/or episodic behavioral condition similar to that of dependent personality disorder. The term is less individually diagnostic and more descriptive of a relationship dynamic. This condition is controversial among psychologists.

In the codependent relationship, one partner mothers the narcissist by taking on the narcissist's responsibilities and picking up their slack. The codependent will go out of their way to take care of the narcissist or any other close relationship. It makes the codependent feel like they are helping when, in reality, they are only hurting the other person or the narcissist. The codependent helps the narcissist stay immature and irresponsible. Most codependent women attract narcissists. Most codependent women did not have some need met in early development.

J.B. Snow says in her book about "12 Types of Women Who Attract Narcissists," one type is the woman who has daddy issues. She says,

" She has daddy issues. A woman often seeks out a partner who is similar in nature to her father, if her father was bossy and intrusive she will seek these traits out in her partner. If her father neglected her in favor of his job and other pursuits, she will chase someone who is also emotionally unavailable to her. She does this in an unconscious effort to win over the father figure who was never there for her. She wants to prove her self-worth to all men.[3]

Thus, women like Wendy can become self-sacrificing. Therefore, be careful when caring for others that you don't forget about loving yourself and the things you love. Ask yourself what you have done for yourself lately? Have you gone to an exercise class? Have you hung out with some of your friends? Did you buy you a new outfit without feeling the guilt because you did not by your partner or children an outfit? I know the narcissist thinks you can't do anything, including buying a cup of coffee apart from them. Their personally says, "it's all about me," but now you see it isn't all about the narcissist. You matter too. So don't stop caring about the narcissist. They need love just like we do, but they don't come first, you do. You can give him a bottle to suck on if you want just don't let him suck the life out of you, Wendy! Take care of yourself. It is alright to be healthy. *You're not crazy; You're dealing with a narcissist.*

4

GIRL, YOU'RE NOT CRAZY

Alright, so has this ever happened to you? You and your partner made plans to go on vacation. You sat down, planned the trip in detail. Noticed I said you sat down with a plan with your partner right there agreeing to everything. That plan included how much the trip would cost, how much of you and your partner's income would take for the trip, and how much time you would have to save money for the trip.

You agreed on the money, the vacation time, when to leave, and you set the date. You are all excited because, finally, you are getting away you think from all of the chaos around you. But, you may not have realized that most of the mess was created by your narcissistic partner.

The time is getting close for your departure. You have been cutting back and saving your part of the income for the trip. So about two weeks before you've planned to leave, you check in with your partner who has not shown any signs of contributing to this long-awaited trip. When you check-in – wait for it. Your charming, narcissistic partner who had you all excited about the trip you were going to take and pay for together looks at you like a deer in headlights.

This is his or her response, "You know I don't have any money." and says, "You know I have to my pay car note, my car insurance, and the mortgage." All this is said with a tone like how dare you ask me about money. You stand there looking like, what just happened? That is because when you had the conversation about the trip several months ago, with this same person standing in front of you calling off the things needing to be paid. This same person knew their bills required payment on the day of the conversation regarding the trip. These bills needed to be paid when the two of you planned and agreed to the trip. You had your car note, your insurance, and other responsibilities just like your partner, but you saved and adjusted for the trip. The interesting thing is the narcissist will have this serious attitude not because they did not know bills needed to be paid. The narcissist is upset because he or she did not bother to save or adjust for the trip. They did not have any serious intensions on providing for the trip. You saw money being wasted when he or she was hanging with the boys, or she was with the girls for the last several months. You saw the new electronic toys he brought or the latest expensive outfits she was buying despite the upcoming trip. The problem is this is not the first time your narcissist partner has pulled this last-minute "I don't have any money" stunt.

Remember when you were talked into buying

the new big-screen television but when the bill came, there was "no money" to pay for it. You had the same kind of conversation with the narcissistic partner who got excited because it was "on-sale." Still, the sale would only last today; therefore, you were encouraged to go out and purchase on credit because your narcissist wanted it, and you wanted to see the person happy. Also, you heard the magic words "I will pay for it," but when the bill came, you got these words, "you know I don't have any money."

At that moment, all you wanted to do, like Wendy in Peter Pan, was to take care of the lost children and his needs. In love, you wanted to believe what your partner said, so you ran out and made the purchase. Now guess what? Because you cared about your credit, and the narcissist does not. You got stuck with the bill while the narcissist enjoys the television and looks at you or even tells you if you are going to be upset, you should not have gone out and brought the big screen. Now you are feeling stupid or crazy for trying to be kind to someone who can care less about the situation they have put you in. That is what a narcissist will do. They rarely consider another person's feelings or consider how what they have done will affect the other person. They are so self-absorb they are only capable of caring about their own agenda, getting the big-screen television. Now their need is met, and you have forgotten your needs due to taking care of the narcissist. The funny thing is all you were trying to do is love the person called, a narcissist.

In love, you may have loaned the narcissist money. However, you did not get it back because, oh, he forgot he has more important responsibilities. In love, you may have sacrificed your time to help the narcissist get his or her dream off the ground. But, when it was your turn, your vision was ignored or not given any attention to by the narcissist. You may have simply picked up the narcissist dry cleaning, but when you asked the same favor, you were given several excuses as to why the narcissist could not oblige you. Because narcissists are good charming others into thinking they have their best interest in mind, people close to them tend to fall for the promises and fantasy they often pour out. Thus causing the other person to feel crazy. Remember the planned vacation the narcissist reneged on? Girl, you are not crazy; you are dealing with a narcissist.

5

YES, YOU HAVE BEEN GASLIT

Have you ever been accused of being jealous or crazy when you've questioned an inappropriate, unacceptable, or negative behavior coming from your narcissistic partner, friend, or family member? Have you been convinced of something you have known to be true, then, all of a sudden, convinced it is not true with the facts sitting in your face? Oh yes, there is more, have you been blamed for the outcome of bad choices your partner, friend, or family has made, but now it is your fault because you should have known things would turn out that way. Were you once confident in what you knew, the decisions you have been making, and where you were going until somehow you were convinced you were wrong? You have been convinced that nobody wants you, everything is just in your imagination, and you are crazy? Are you second-guessing your thoughts, actions, and outcomes of things you use to know to be accurate and sure of, but now you are not sure of anything? If so, you may have been gaslit. In an April 30, 2017 post written by Preston Ni, M.S.B.A. on the *7 Stages of Gaslighting in a Relationship* in Psychology Today article he says,

> Gaslighting is a form of persistent manipulation and brainwashing that causes the victim to doubt her or himself, and ultimately lose her or his own sense of perception, identity, and self-worth. The term is derived from the 1944 film *Gaslight,* in which a husband tries to convince his wife that she's insane by causing her to question herself and her reality.[1]

That is what a narcissist will do. They will unapologetically cause you to think you are crazy. They will convince you that you are wrong and they are right. They will go as far as tell you that you are crazy when you attempt to present them with facts. They will create an outrageous story with incredible details to convince you of something that is not real or has no truth to it. They will go to any extreme to save face when they have totally messed something up. They have no problem telling you a lie to get their way and convince you that you have agreed to something you did not. They will use put-downs to make themselves look good, and another person, especially their significant other look bad. They will convince you the sky is orange when you are looking at a clear blue sky, and the worst part of it you have allowed them to do so by listening to their nonsense. You didn't get there on your own. Narcissists are good at wearing people down. They have a way of out talking others and coming up with so many different stories in one conversation the victim being gaslit by the narcissist either gives in to the story or go as far as to believe the lie because the stories are so convincing. That is why so many partners of narcissists are walking around, saying they feel like they are losing their minds. In reality, they are being brainwashed to believe something that they know is not true. They are holding their head trying to make sense of the last story they were convinced to believe.

This doesn't just happen on television or at the movies. This happens to everyday people who are in a relationship with a narcissist. It occurs when a person's gut is yelling their partner is cheating. All the signs are there. The partner stays out all night, doesn't answering the phone while staying out, comes in with the smell of other women on him, and refuses to show you any type of intimacy. The partner goes off in corners to talk on the phone and hangs up soon as you walk in the room. The best part, for the starring actor, is when you confront the cheater. They become enraged to make you think you are crazy by saying the following; "you are jealous of everyone I talk too," then the popular one, "you know you are the one cheating," and hear it comes, "Oh my God, you are just crazy." Then you start to question all the signs. You retreat because the narcissist has been so adamant about not cheating, acting as though you are really losing it. All which causes low self-esteem to kick in. You start to think, "Maybe I am crazy," and "I might be wrong." Because you are worn down and confused, you begin to believe what the narcissist has told you to be true. While everything you suspected, you find out to be true. The narcissist had gaslit you unto believing his or her lie. Soon as you start to second guess yourself, the narcissist has gained control over your thoughts. You have been made to feel like you are crazy, but you are not crazy, you are dealing with a narcissist!

The whole purpose of gaslighting is to confuse and manipulate its victim into believing a lie or something that is not real. Then by the time you figure out what just happened to you, it is too late. The narcissist now believes their own lie and knows you are now second-guessing yourself, so in the future, you will not be sure of what is real. Thus causing you to shrink back from even questioning future lies or things you suspect to be false or know to be true. It can happen to the best of us, especially when we genuinely care about the narcissistic partner, friend, and or family member. The narcissist has gotten his needs met by enjoying his affair. The narcissist will continue having affairs because you don't want to be accused of cheating or feeling crazier than you already feel.

Now you are left scratching your head, trying to figure how did you get manipulated into paying for a television? Or, how did you get manipulated into going along with the narcissist's affairs? I will tell you how. Your partner can be very charming and believable at the time. I don't care how many lies they have told you. They have a way of convincing others by promising to do something they have no intension of following through. They have a way of making you think you are crazy when they want to manipulate you into thinking something is true when it is not.

Since you are not self-absorbed like the narcissist, you can't imagine anyone going to the extremes the narcissist will go to by lying to convince you. So you believed the lie. Once the narcissist does not follow through on a promise, they will then convince you it was your idea, not theirs in the first place. Then, when they can't see their way out of something, they will make you think you are crazy to get what they want from a television to a divorce. In reality, you are not crazy; you are dealing with are narcissist that has gaslit you. The whole purpose of gaslighting is to deliberately convince another person their perception is off and that they are crazy.

6

TRUST YOUR GUT

I recently did something I very seldom do. While leaving the grocery store that I had stopped by after I had gotten off work, a man approached me in the parking lot offering to help with my bags. My perception is usually pretty good about this type of situation. There are not men just hanging around parking lots waiting to help with loading groceries unless they want something. I work with those who struggle with addiction, so I am usually pretty good with the signs. My gut told me by looking at the man who was profusely sweating that he had a problem with some type of addiction. Being tired and just ready to get home, I waited for the man to ask for money. Then he says, "Ma'am, I am hungry and have not eaten all day. Do you happen to have a couple of dollars, so I get something to eat?" He pointed at a nearby chicken restaurant. Usually, I would just blow the person off, or I would offer to buy the person food just in case they were really hungry. However, me being tired and against my gut belief that he was hustling me to do something other than eating, I gave in and gave him money. It was only a couple of dollars; however, as I pulled off to looked back to see if the man would head to the food place he had pointed to when asking for the money, he did not. However, he did as my gut suspected he proceeded to his next victim.

My eyes also caught him as he pulled out a hand full of money I suspect he had gotten from prior victims to add with what he had gotten from me. I was irritated for a second and felt like going back to say something to him, but what for? My gut had already told me what he was doing when he first approached me saying,

"Can I help with your groceries" my gut said, "here comes someone to hustle me for money to get high." People with alcohol and or substance abuse problems tend to have or develop a narcissistic disorder. They become self-absorbed with their addiction. Their ultimate goal in life becomes getting high on drugs or alcohol. Their addiction becomes their priority, and everything else takes a back seat. The addiction can become so intense that the addict is willing to lie like the young man in the parking lot, steal, and in a few cases, kill to feed their habit. Being addicted to anything can change a person's behavior. When it comes to a narcissist, it is easier to lie, steal, cheat, and possibly kill. Why? Because they cannot care about how others feel or to be empathetic to those they hurt. Therefore when they ask for money to get a car fixed to get to work or to pay a bill before their lights get turned off or even like the man in the parking lot using the old, "I am hungry" trick, it does not bother them that you may have given them money that you needed for yourself or your own self-care. They will lie without remorse.

What causes people to give in to the narcissist when your gut is telling you they are feeding you a lie? Most people don't think like a narcissist. Most people think other people are good honest citizens until they prove they are not. When you are an honest, caring person, your mind does not think like a narcissist. Therefore, when you are first approached by the narcissist with their heart-touching story, your first instinct may be to believe them. I mean, who would lie and say that their children are hungry when they know they are not? A narcissist would. Who would convince a person they are in love with you and want to marry you but is not. A narcissist would.

Who would not stop what they are doing to comfort you after you just poured your heart out about your dying loved one? A narcissist would not. Who would ask for your last dime to meet a want, not a need, and not pay it back? The true narcissist would. Then they will have the nerve to come back later with an elaborate story about needing your help again. Your gut and history tell you "don't do it"; however, because their mother just die or their dog just died, you ignore your gut and give in. In your mind, you might be thinking, who would ever be this insensitive? The narcissist would. Understand in the mind of the narcissist; they believe everybody behaves like that, what's the big deal?

Why do people not follow their gut and give into their lie? It is sometimes hard to believe a person can be that selfish and unsympathetic. Therefore we provide the narcissist the benefit of the doubt versus trusting our gut. Who said you have to give others the benefit of the doubt, especially if the person is known to be a liar? What tends to be more accurate when it comes to what your gut is telling you or the benefit of the doubt? I am not saying you don't give people a chance. Giving people a chance or trusting another is what the benefit of the doubt is until the trust is broken. However, if you know someone to be a liar, it is foolish to ignore your gut when it is telling you, run Forest run. With the narcissist, you will see a pattern of them always wanting to come first, having their needs met first, their plan is first, and your need is not important. You can usually tell when they start off talking that they are getting ready to give you a story that will benefit them and not you. You can generally tell when something they are saying is not true by your gut feeling. You might not have all the evidence in front of you yet. What you will always have is your gut feeling. If you are of the faith, as I am, you will know the spirit within you is telling you something's not right. It would be in your best interest not to make a quick decision as I did in the parking lot or any other situation when you are caught off guard. You do have the right not to decide at that moment; however, the narcissist will try to get you to make a quick decision. They are so manipulative they know if you take time to think you will figure out you are being manipulated or lied to. They are usually fast talkers, and they have read you long before the conversation. They are prepared. You typically are not. Take time to think, especially if you know you are dealing with a narcissist. Pay attention to the funny thing that happens in your stomach when the narcissist is feeding you a story that is going to cost you because it will cost you. For those who are spiritual, and understand spiritual things, know that that thing happening in your stomach is how the spirit of God works. So again, I encourage you to trust your gut in your daily life, especially when dealing with a narcissist.

7

NARCISSISTIC PERSONALITY DISORDER AND ADDICTION

Just like there are many people in the world with narcissistic personality disorder (generally men), unfortunately, there are many people today who struggle with substance abuse disorders and alcoholism. If you happen to be in a close relationship with someone who is struggling with substance abuse or alcoholism, you know how hard that can be on the relationship. Some of the same characteristics of narcissists are present with those with substance abuse disorders.

The person suffering from substance abuse and

the person with a narcissistic personality can both have the same characters such as their inability to be empathetic with others and their failure to connect with others emotionally. Those with substance abuse disorders tend to care more about feeding their addiction then caring about how their life of addiction affects those who care about them. Just like the narcissistic personality lacks empathy due to their inability to connect emotionally with others, the addict becomes numb to others' feelings due to being self-absorbed with feeding their drug of choice. The narcissistic personality and the substance abuser both are good at lying and manipulating others to get what they want.

Those diagnosed with a substance abuse disorder are considered to be one as having a "disease," unlike those diagnosed with a narcissistic personality disorder. However, both substance abuse disorders and narcissistic disorders can be treated with behavioral therapy. If you or if anyone you happen to be in a relationship with is effected by narcissistic personality disorder or a substance abuse disorder, please understand you can't do it alone. Neither of you can cure the person with the disorder. However, you can get help and encourage the other person to get the help they need. There are many behavioral therapy programs in most cities and or states equipped to help treat both disorders.

The nationwide, *24-hour Drug Abuse Helpline*, is **866-948-9865**.

8

TRUST MUST BE EARNED... NOT!

It has been said trust must be earned. However, as I was listening to one of Evan Marc Katz's "Love Me" podcast, he shared on the falsehood of that statement. He suggested trust is not earned; it is first given. He likened earning trust as being found guilty before being proved innocent. Since trust is something that is freely given, once the trust is broken, then it should be taken away. It used to be my thought that trust must be earned. However, when a friend, family member, or partner borrows money and says they are going to pay it back, there is a level of trust involved in the beginning. When the money is loaned, I expect the money will be returned. That is until the friend, family member, or partner proves otherwise by not repaying the loan, thus causing the trust to be lost. In the case of loaning money, it is not normal for a person to just give out loans to people they don't know or trust. The trust usually comes first; then, if the money is not returned, the trust is lost.

Therefore we should be careful not to put everyone in the same trustworthy category. There may be people in our lives that have a history of not paying back the money. Therefore it is not wise to put your trust in them. That does not mean you will not give them money or the people you love. You just give with the understanding from history that if you give that person your money, you most likely will not get it back. Why, because the trust that was initially given is now lost. The person has proven not to be trustworthy. To not trust someone else because someone from your past or someone that has wronged you recently is not fair. That is when you start to develop a mindset that all people are liars, and all people will not pay you back. In being fair, why not just label the person or persons who have earned the title of being untrustworthy, a liar, or whatever the case may be. The same thing often happens with all men are labelled as cheaters, because a couple of people in your past may have cheated on you. Or the people you are drawn to are cheaters. That does mean you can't trust other men or women who are honest. You will never have a healthy or successful relationship thinking that way about all men or women. To think all men cheat is not fair to the faithful men. Neither is it appropriate for the new man or woman to pay for what the men or women in the past have done. However, if you are in a relationship with a cheater, that person has broken trust before. Therefore trust should be taken away and proven (earned) because it should not be given to the untrustworthy person. So does trust have to be earned? Not at all when it comes to someone who has not given you a reason not to trust them.

9

SETTING BOUNDARIES

It is absolutely necessary to establish boundaries when you have identified a partner, friend, family member, coworker, or neighbor as a narcissist. The importance of setting boundaries is to allow you to set limits. The narcissist usually knows no bounds when it comes to what they will ask of you to meet his or her needs. They will start with your time, then your money, and anything that will benefit his or her needs.

Since the narcissist does not have respect for another person's time, money, or their needs, including having no boundaries when it comes to doing whatever it takes to get what they want including your attention. If limits are set with the narcissist you can establish how much time, money and their needs you are willing to give attention to. The limits are to help protect you. A narcissist will never acknowledge limits when you state them. It is up to you to enforce the limits.

For example, when it comes to your time you can be in the middle of something you consider of importance to you like your job, your favorite hobby or your children. However, the narcissist will interrupt you to meet his or her need. If you try to put the narcissist off by asking can they wait or can it be done later, you will get a, no.

The narcissist will either manipulate you with guilt or accuse you of being the reason they have the problem in the first place. If that doesn't work the narcissist will go as far as tears or throwing a temper tantrum to manipulate you into taking care of their problem. They are such good manipulators.

If you are not good at setting boundaries by the

time they get finish giving you all of the drama about their needs you would have forgotten what you were doing for yourself. Now you have lost interest in your need due to being worn down with all of the drama that you have just encountered with the narcissist.

You may be willing to give in just to get rid the narcissist so they can move on and you can get back to your needs. If you can remember what your need was. Once they have gotten what they wanted they have made a mental note that wearing you down worked. Don't feel bad if it has happened to you multiple times. It has happened to the best of us. Especially if you are good hearted by nature. They target those who are nice and are givers.

Just know you need to set some boundaries to limit the narcissist's shenanigans. Most of the time before one realizes they have to set boundaries, it has never crossed their mind that a human being could be so self-absorbed and manipulating.

Most caring people don't think like this. However, the more you give in without setting boundaries the more the narcissist will take advantage, and enjoy life at your expense.

The best way to set boundaries with the narcissist is by having a game plan and sticking to it. Talk to the narcissist about what you are willing to do or not do when interrupted with what their agenda and emergencies (It will always be urgent with them).

When it comes to your time you may want to remind the narcissist your time is just as important as theirs. If you have friends or hobbies you like spending time with, determine how much time you would like to spend with them and stick with. It is your planned time unless you see the narcissist needs to go to the hospital. So enjoy your time.

Do the same for the narcissist. Determine how much time you would like to spend with your partner, friends, and family. Make sure you take time for yourself. Of course you can be flexible.

However, be aware when it always turns out to be about the narcissist's need for your time. If you have a partner that wants all of your time, money and attention, set some boundaries. You have to work therefore that time is off limits unless what you deem to be an emergency.

If money is borrowed from you by the narcissist make sure you have a clear agreement on when money should be paid back. In severe cases you may need a signed contract. If you have planned to spend time with your friends outside of your partner, take that time without apology. You may even need some alone time to yourself, take time to yourself but communicate that is what you are doing.

For example, when he or she always goes out with his or her friends but does not call, returns home late, and making you feeling alone. The way you are feeling will need to be communicated.

The narcissist, because they are self-absorbed may not see hanging out with his or her friends all the time until late as a problem. Without you communicating how that makes you feel the narcissist may not get that it leaves you feeling lonely. That is not balance and can be a problem.

You can decide what you are willing to tolerate. Remember the narcissist is self-absorbed and mainly thinks about his or her own needs. Therefore you must be clear about what you expect and are willing or not willing to do. You must hold the narcissist accountable for his or her negative behavior. Setting boundaries will help with setting the necessary limits within the relationship with the narcissist. When those boundaries are not respected or crossed, there should be reasonable consequences.

Communication of those boundaries may need to be articulated over and over again. The narcissist will tend to get convenient amnesia when it comes to promises they made and don't want to keep. They will agree upon certain things when they are in a good mood. Keep reinforcing the agreed-upon boundaries because once you give the narcissist an inch, they will take several miles.

It will help you to remember excellent communication with the narcissist, setting boundaries and holding to your decisions. You almost have to treat the narcissist like children, teaching them what is expected of them. You will either train them to respect you and your time, or they will train you to allow their disrespect. It is true. People will only do what we allow them to do. Set some boundaries.

10

SEEK TO UNDERSTAND

Understanding the narcissist will be substantial especially when you are married to a narcissist; the person is a significant relative (parent, child, or sibling) and or a significant friend. Understanding that the narcissist sometimes has a personality disorder such as antisocial personality disorder will help those in relationship with the narcissist know how their brain may be wired. This disorder comes with symptoms such as not being able to show empathy, connect emotionally, and showing no regard for right or wrong. The antisocial personality's brain is wired that way.

Sometimes without counseling or psychotherapy, the narcissist or antisocial personality usually does not change or get better. Even with therapy, the narcissist may still have a hard time seeing others' needs and focusing on just his or her. It can be hard to deal with the narcissist without seeming judgmental of their selfish behavior; therefore, I would encourage those in relationship with a narcissist to try the following:

1. Seek to understand the mental and emotional challenges of the narcissist. The narcissist does not have the emotional or mental capacity to care about others because they are self-absorbed. Remember, it is usually all about them first. Therefore, I would not put too much stock in expecting the narcissist to meet your emotional needs or make your needs a priority without them looking for something in return. You will most likely be setting yourself up for disappointment if you

do. Unless there is a mind to change, or therapy involved, to expect the narcissist to put you first automatically may not happen.

2. Understand because of the way the narcissist's brain is wired; they are usually not capable of feeling emotional when you are in a crisis or require sympathy. For example, if you come to the narcissist tearful and hurting due to a loss or some traumatic experience, you may get a blank stare or look, not a hug. Instead of getting angry, you will do well to remember the narcissists are just not very sympathetic or compassionate. Even if they show signs of sympathy be on guard, there may be a motive behind it. Amazingly the same crisis can happen to him or her, and they will expect total empathy or sympathy. They can have a traumatic loss or crisis and expect you to be understanding and empathetic, but

know it may not be reciprocated when you are hurting.

3. Understand just because the narcissist has a hard time feeling emotions, and having compassion for others does not mean that there is something wrong with you. Therefore when the narcissist accuses you of being too sensitive or emotional, understand that is from their perspective and their struggle with expressing feelings and emotions. That is the narcissist's stuff, not yours. You may even want to encourage the narcissist not to make negative comments or statements when it comes to how you express your feelings and emotions. Pointing out the fact your feelings are yours and that you are entitled to them may help the narcissist see things from a different perspective other than their own. Because they have difficulty expressing their feelings and emotions, they should not judge those

that have feelings. Explaining to the narcissist how they make you feel may go over better than just pointing out how big of a jerk they are or sometimes seem to be.

4. Understand with the narcissist often, without professional help, will have a hard time processing his or her feelings and emotions. Understanding others' feelings and emotions would be hard if they can't handle their own. Therefore unless you are a person of great patience and know-how to set proper boundaries, it will be challenging to stay in a healthy relationship with a narcissist. You may find yourself being offended, often depending on how selfish the narcissist in your life exhibits. However, there is hope of surviving a relationship with a narcissist. It will be vital that you know how to set proper boundaries and stick to them.

11

SURVIVING THE NARCISSIST

In light of the fact, the narcissist may be your spouse, parent, son, daughter, or your boss, surviving in the relationship is essential. The truth is, you may not want to up and leave your spouse, the father or mother of your children, cut off your beloved son or daughter, and or the person who writes your paycheck. However, it would be helpful to figure out how to survive the self-centered, self-absorb, and hard to deal with a narcissist. If you have a spouse who lacks empathy or a boss who is constantly criticizing you and children, that is all about them, singing me, me, me, you need a plan.

If you have a parent who is a narcissist, that parent may expect you to drop everything every time they call. It will not matter if you have a spouse, children, and a job that needs tending to. Remember, the narcissistic personality is self-absorbed, therefore it is all about them. You may have a hard time setting boundaries without feelings of guilt when it comes to a parent. However, setting healthy boundaries will help free children of narcissistic parents from their constant manipulation and control. Children, especially adult children, have a right to their own life with their family, friends, and things they enjoy doing for themselves. Even the scripture says, "a man shall leave his father and his mother, and shall cleave to unto his wife" (Genesis 2:24). At the same time, honor those parents with carved out time to spend with them for they are important. When you began putting their needs before your own needs and the needs of what is important to you like your family, your children, and things you value, that can pose a problem, including resentment. By all means, be there for your parents but not by way of manipulation and control.

When your spouse only cares about his or her needs, that is when you must decide how much self-centeredness you are going to tolerate. Remember, you must define and set healthy limits. If you are a giver and your narcissistic spouse is a taker, try not to expect the narcissist to come baring gifts, unless he or she wants something in return. Usually, they will want something in return. Giving up his or her time and volunteering to help is often not a given. You will need a clear understanding of what the narcissist is capable of and or willing to do for you. Here are two different examples. The first is when the narcissist is incapable of being there emotionally. When dealing with a spouse or a partner who is unable to comfort you when you are hurting or grieving a loss, while it is essential to share your feelings, be prepared for the possible nonchalant response. If you have a friend or family member who you know would be more supportive and compassionate, you may do well by turning to that person for comfort. Feeling compassionate in your time of need may not be one of your narcissistic partner's strength.

The second is the narcissist's inability to give freely. If he or she was not willing to buy you a birthday card for your birthday or a gift at Christmas, that might not be on his or her radar as well.

Say Christmas is one of your favorite holidays. It has been your tradition to celebrate with those close to you by exchanging gifts or buying gifts for your loved ones or children. You may go all out or make expensive purchases. It does not matter if the cost is big or small; you like the gift of giving during the holiday season. You purchase your narcissistic spouse a gift. You look forward to the excitement on his or her face because you know it was something he or she has been talking about for some time. Christmas day comes, and you can't wait to make him or her happy with the gift. The gift is opened and with a big smile on his or her face, thanks to you being thoughtful enough to buy something he or she wanted and will enjoy.

You wait for the exchange. However, there is nothing. It is not reciprocated. You may get a story from him or her saying they did not have time to pick up a gift or any enough money to buy you a gift. The narcissist may even say he or she did not have enough money to get you a gift. They got their mother a present. Either story will leave one feeling unimportant due to the fact the narcissist did not take the time or the money to make an effort. That is not the end of the story. The same thing happened on your anniversary, Valentine's Day and Mother's or Father's Day. The narcissist may or may not have asked you to buy the gift. Therefore, you may want to have a conversation to avoid the narcissist's insensitive behavior from happening again.

You can ask the narcissist if they would like to exchange gifts at Christmas or anniversaries with a set limit. Remember, the narcissist may voluntarily offer a small gift with the motive of getting a more significant one in return. Set your Limits. If you have a conversation and commitment, you may avoid being disappointed by giving without receiving. This is all about setting realistic expectations for yourself and the narcissist. It is alright to protect yourself from future disappointment. Make it clear that they do not have to exchange gifts, but if they decide not to, there will not be a gift from you. The narcissist does not mind receiving, but giving may be a struggle for the narcissist.

There can be other agreements made, but the first thing one has to remember when dealing with the narcissist. Due to their self-absorb personality, they can be very selfish and self-centered. Expecting the narcissist to empathize or show compassion readily is just not one of their traits. Therefore make sure you communicate your expectations and agreements. When they are not met, have a conversation. When expectations are met, say thank you. It may encourage the narcissist to continue with positive behavior. You may not fully know what is behind the narcissist childish behavior. It could be a scared little boy that was not nurtured by a parent or both parents. Or the little girl that was ignored or did not get the attention she deserved. There may be other personality disorders going on that has not been diagnosed. Your compassion may shed some light on what it means to care about others. Whatever you do or don't do, just know that you are not crazy, *you may be dealing with a narcissist.*

EPILOGUE

In conclusion, a narcissistic personality disorder is a personality disorder with long-term patterns of abnormal behavior characterized by exaggerated feelings of self-importance, excessive need for admiration, and a lack of empathy. Just as the young man in the Peter Pan story, the narcissist cannot grow up or engage in behaviors associate with adulthood. The narcissist would prefer to make time playing overtaking responsibility by working. Women with personalities like Wendy, in the Peter Pan story, like taking on the role of a mother, usually fall into the trap of caring for the Peter Pan's in her life. It can be her spouse, her son, or a friend. If there is a need, Wendy is usually there to fulfill the need. She is good at putting others before herself because of her loyalty to those of whom she cares about. Caring people like Wendy just need to understand it is alright to take care of themselves first. Self-care is one of the best ways to survive in life. Put your mask on first then help if you can without hurting you.

Most importantly, women like Wendy who care for and are sometimes taken advantage of by the narcissist needs someone to remind them, *Girl you're not crazy, you're are dealing with a narcissist.* That person dealing with the narcissistic personality needs to know they may have been manipulated into believing something that is not true. The victim of a narcissist needs to know that, yes, you have been played and, no, the narcissist is not going to pay. The victim needs to know they were not crazy to make any agreements with the narcissist, besides who would have thought someone you care about would leave you hanging with a bill, without remorse. Understand, *Girl, you're not crazy, you're dealing with a narcissist.*

In the future, when dealing with a narcissist, it will be important to trust your gut and the red flags waving in front of you. This is especially important if you have been tricked by a narcissist before. When in doubt, don't give a quick answer or an immediate response. Allow yourself time to think. When people you trust and love tell you don't do it, don't do it. When that voice in your head says, don't do it, don't. You don't owe anyone the benefit of the doubt. You will be the one who pays for not listening to your gut.

Setting healthy boundaries will help to stop people like the narcissist from crossing your limits. Because narcissists usually know no boundaries, it will be up to you to set them to protect yourself from the narcissists crossing your limits. Understanding that some narcissists have a personality disorder will help with your knowledge of their lack of emotional support and their inability to be empathetic. This, however, does not give the narcissist a pass. It is just a reminder of how the narcissist's brain is wired. With therapy, you may be able to have a better relationship with the narcissist if he or she is willing. It is also a helpful reminder; you are not crazy because your perspective may be different when it comes to feelings and emotions. Because narcissists are people in close relationship to us in some way of life, we must learn how to survive in the relationship. In surviving a relationship with a narcissist, setting healthy boundaries, practicing self-care, and good communication is the key. You must define the limits; the narcissist will not. Remember to be kind and helpful to your narcissistic parents, your partner, your children, and friends. However, make sure you take care of yourself first. Put the mask on you first. The narcissist will quickly put their mask on first and will call you crazy for not putting yours on if you keep them from drowning. Just always remember you're not crazy, you're dealing with a narcissist.

For more information on the narcissist, refer to the books and YouTube videos available about the Narcissist. Some of my favorites are included in references.

ENDNOTES

1. What is a Narcissist?

1. Wikipedia   -
   https://en.wikipedia.org/wiki/Narcissistic_personal-
   ity_disorder
2. YouTube; Bishop R.C. Blakes, The Mind Games
   Narcissists Plays In Relationships - https://www.
   youtube.com/watch?v=4pCaiBqV7bk

2. Peter Pan, the Narcissist

1. Wikipedia, Peter Pan syndrome - https://en.
   wikipedia.org/wiki/Peter_Pan_syndrome

3. Are You a Wendy?

1. Step to Health, The Wendy Syndrome: Caring for
   Others and Neglecting Yourself, November 30, 2019
   - https://steptohealth.com/wendy-syndrome-caring-
   others-neglecting/
2. Wikipedia, Codependency - https://en.wikipedia.
   org/wiki/Codependency
3. 12 Types of Women Who Attract Narcissists,
   J.B. Snow

5. Yes, You Have Been Gaslit

1. Psychology Today, *7 Stages of Gaslighting in a Relationship* by Preston Ni, M.S.B.A.

CPSIA information can be obtained
at www.ICGtesting.com
Printed in the USA
BVHW040507080720
583187BV00006B/661

9 781950 719402